Power of the Spoken Word
Study Manual

Corey Russell

Copyright 2025–Corey Russell

All rights reserved. This book is protected by the copyright laws of the United States of America. This book may not be copied or reprinted for commercial gain or profit. The use of short quotations or occasional page copying for personal or group study is permitted and encouraged. Permission will be granted upon request. Unless otherwise indicated, all scripture quotations are taken from the *King James Version* of the Bible. Used by permission. All rights reserved.

All emphasis within Scripture quotations is the author's own. Please note that Harrison House's publishing style capitalizes certain pronouns in Scripture that refer to the Father, Son, and Holy Spirit, and may differ from some publishers' styles. Take note that the name satan and related names are not capitalized. We choose not to acknowledge him, even to the point of violating grammatical rules.

Harrison House P.O. Box 310, Shippensburg, PA 17257-0310

This book and all other Harrison House's books are available at Christian bookstores and distributors worldwide.

Reach us on the Internet: www.harrisonhouse.com.

ISBN 13 TP: 978-1-6675-1185-6

ISBN 13 eBook: 978-1-6675-1186-3

Contents

1. Awakening to Our Identity ... 1
2. Who Are You Talking To? ... 9
3. What Do You Want, God? ... 17
4. The Revelation of Intercession ... 25
5. Old Testament Intercessors, Part 1 ... 33
6. Old Testament Intercessors, Part 2 ... 41
7. Jesus—His Intercession and Our Union with Him ... 49
8. Teach Us to Pray ... 57
9. The Furnace of Prayer ... 65
10. Birthing Revival ... 73
11. Where Is This Going? ... 81
12. What Does This Look Like Today? ... 89

About the Author ... 97
About the Publisher ... 99

Chapter 1

Awakening to Our Identity

"Even them I will bring to My holy mountain, and make them joyful in My house of prayer. Their burnt offerings and their sacrifices will be accepted on My altar; for My house shall be called a house of prayer for all nations." (Isaiah 56:7, NKJV)

A man knelt in his hotel room in Cairo, Egypt, during a mission trip meant to connect him with God's heart for the poor. But it was not just poverty he encountered—it was the voice of God, thundering into the room with a declaration that would alter the course of his life and ministry: *"I will change the understanding and the expression of Christianity in the whole earth in one generation."* Immobilized under the thick presence of the Lord, this man began to understand that God was initiating a global transformation—not only in how the world perceives the Church but in how the Church perceives itself.

The phrase *"understanding"* referred to how unbelievers would come to view the Church as relevant and powerful. The *"expression"* pointed to how believers would return to operating with divine purpose and purity. At the core of this change were four heart standards that God longed to restore: intercession, holiness, offerings to the poor, and prophecy. These are not optional features of the Church; they are foundational callings that have been resisted, especially from within. And among them, intercession is first.

As prayer and worship have exploded across the globe—from 24/7 houses of prayer to solar-lit gatherings in the wilderness—the Church is awakening to a glorious truth: Jesus is not only our great Evangelist; He is the eternal Intercessor. God is stirring the nations to respond to His invitation. Even in the darkest corners of the earth, prayer is rising like incense, echoing the ancient prophecy of Malachi: *"My name shall be great among the Gentiles."*

But before there can be global transformation, there must be personal revelation. This chapter issues a bold call to every believer: reclaim your identity. You are not just a member of a church—you are a priest. You are an intercessor. Will you allow God to redefine how you see yourself and embrace the glorious burden of intimacy and authority in prayer?

Focus Point

"Even them I will bring to My holy mountain, and make them joyful in My house of prayer.... For My house shall be called a house of prayer for all nations." (Isaiah 56:7, NKJV)

This verse uncovers the very heartbeat of God. His desire is not simply for obedient servants or gifted ministers, but for joyful intercessors. God's house is defined not by preaching, healing, or activity—but by prayer. And not just any prayer, but joyful communion with Him. He longs to gather us into intimacy and partnership through the language of prayer, restoring our identity and authority as intercessors in the earth.

Main Theme

This chapter unveils the reality that God is shifting the global expression of Christianity through the restoration of intercession. This restoration isn't reserved for a few loud voices in the back room—it's for every believer. The first barrier we must overcome is identity confusion. We think prayer is for the spiritually elite, but Scripture tells us every believer is a priest. Pride, unbelief, and spiritual ignorance have silenced our voices, but God is removing the veil. Through Christ, we are already seated in heavenly places, already brought near, already equipped to commune. God is awakening His Church, beginning with you and me, to stand before Him and release His will on earth.

"To be a believer is to be an intercessor."

Key Scriptures

- *"Even them I will bring to My holy mountain, and make them joyful in My house of prayer."* (Isaiah 56:7, NKJV)
- *"But you are a chosen generation, a royal priesthood, a holy nation, His own special*

people, that you may proclaim the praises of Him who called you out of darkness into His marvelous light." (1 Peter 2:9, NKJV)
- *"And have made us kings and priests to our God; and we shall reign on the earth."* (Revelation 5:10, NKJV)

KEY POINTS

- **God Will Change the Understanding and Expression of Christianity** The Church is being redefined. God declared that in one generation, He would change how the world sees the Church and how the Church sees itself.
- **Intercession Is for Everyone** Prayer is not the ministry of a few—it's the identity of all believers. To be saved is to be called into the ministry of intercession.
- **We're Moving from the Back Room to the Front Line** Intercession is no longer a hidden ministry. God is bringing it to the forefront of churches, mission movements, and individual callings.
- **Barriers Must Fall: Pride, Unbelief, Ignorance, and Apathy** The biggest obstacles to prayer are within us. Pride tells us we don't need help, unbelief tells us God won't listen, and apathy keeps us silent.
- **The House of Prayer Will Be a House of Joy** Prayer is not drudgery—it's a place of joy. God promises to make us joyful in His house, not bored or weary.
- **Jesus Cleansed the Temple—Twice** At both the beginning and end of His ministry, Jesus cleansed the temple. Why? Because God's house had become a marketplace instead of a sanctuary of prayer.
- **We Are a Kingdom of Priests** Heaven's vision is clear—Revelation 5 says the Church will recognize herself as a kingdom of priests. Our calling is not second-hand. It is the original design.

JOURNALING QUESTIONS

Journaling in light of this chapter invites readers to reflect deeply on how they view themselves and prayer. The truths presented here challenge the notion that intercession is for a few and affirm that it is the birthright of every believer. As readers write, they will begin to uncover false beliefs, prideful independence, and the lies that have prevented them from stepping into their true role. The act of journaling gives space for God to speak, convict, and call them into a lifestyle of communion and authority.

By engaging with the journaling questions, readers can expect the Lord to speak about their priestly identity. They may recognize where they've relied on self, where they've misunderstood God's desire, or where they've felt unworthy. This section becomes a mirror that reflects both the reader's current walk and the high calling of God for their life. It's not about perfection—it's about response. Through reflection, they will begin to rise as joyful intercessors.

Redefining Prayer

How has my definition or experience of prayer shaped the way I engage with God?

_____
_____
_____
_____
_____
_____
_____

Barrier Breakdown

Which of the four barriers—pride, unbelief, lack of identity, or feeling ineffective—has most hindered my prayer life?

_____
_____
_____
_____
_____
_____

My Place at the Table

What does it mean to truly believe that I have access to God's throne as a priest?

The Zeal of Jesus

What areas of my life need to be cleansed and reordered so that they reflect Jesus' passion for the house of prayer?

Agreement with Heaven

How can I begin living as someone who agrees with heaven's view of my identity and calling?

Actionable Steps

Cultivate a Daily Prayer Habit
Begin each day by simply whispering phrases of love, thanks, or petition to God. Don't wait for perfection—just begin.

Equip Your Mind with Scripture
Memorize Isaiah 56:7, 1 Peter 2:9, and Revelation 5:10 this week. Let these verses define who you are in Christ.

Engage with Community Prayer
Join or initiate a prayer meeting—even if it's just with one other person. Push past the resistance and step into corporate intercession.

Personal Reflection

As you take in the truths of this chapter, ask yourself: Have I been living as a priest, or have I allowed my circumstances, insecurities, or traditions to silence my voice before God? Maybe you've believed that prayer is for the "spiritual elite" or for someone else in the church, but not for you. Maybe you've felt disqualified by your past or intimidated by your weakness. But in this moment, God is extending a divine invitation to you. You were made for intimacy. You were made for intercession. You were made for Him.

Surrender isn't a feeling—it's a decision. As you respond to this chapter, I encourage you to talk to God in simple, honest words. Offer your heart again. Let Him reframe how you see yourself. Let go of striving and press into receiving. He is calling you back to the original design: to live as a friend of God and a priest in His house.

Have I accepted God's invitation to live as an intercessor? Am I willing to let go of self-sufficiency and embrace joyful communion? Will I take my place in the house of prayer and partner with God for His purposes in the earth?

_____
_____
_____
_____

Closing Prayer: *Lord, You have called me to something far greater than I've ever imagined. You have not asked me to perform, but to draw near. You have not invited me into works, but into Your presence. I receive Your truth that I am a priest and an intercessor. Break every barrier of pride, unbelief, and passivity in me. Let zeal for Your house consume me, and make me joyful in prayer. Teach me to stand before You in confidence and release Your kingdom through my words. I say yes to the call. Amen.*

Chapter 2

Who Are You Talking To?

"For from the rising of the sun, even to its going down, My name shall be great among the Gentiles; in every place incense shall be offered to My name, and a pure offering; for My name shall be great among the nations," says the Lord of hosts. (Malachi 1:11, NKJV)

While standing in front of a mirror in a bathroom in Basel, Switzerland, preparing to speak at a prayer conference, I heard the Lord interrupt my thoughts. "I have two questions for you," He said. The first thundered in my spirit with holy force: *"Who in the world do you think you're talking to?"* I stood frozen, suddenly aware of the gravity behind those words. It wasn't condemnation—it was invitation. God was confronting me not to shame me, but to realign me. That moment was a divine disruption. And the revelation that followed has never left me.

This question didn't point to a need for better prayer techniques. It was about perception. Who do I believe God is? How do I see Him? What comes into my mind when I say, "Father"? The lack of power and intimacy in many prayer lives can be traced to an inaccurate view of God. If we think He's distant, disinterested, or burdened by our needs, we'll never approach Him with confidence. But if we see Him as great, glorious, kind, and near, prayer becomes the natural overflow of our lives.

From Genesis to Revelation, God reveals Himself as the One who longs to be known. He is not hiding. He's beckoning us to gaze upon His beauty, trust in His strength, and anchor our identity in His unchanging nature. When we truly see who He is, our hearts awaken to love, our prayers ignite with faith, and our souls find rest in His presence. Confidence in prayer is not rooted in our effort—it is rooted in our view of God.

So the real question remains: *Who do you say that He is?* Your answer will define not only your theology but your entire life. You will never pray boldly until you believe rightly. Let's allow the Spirit of God to renew our minds, elevate our vision, and anchor our prayers in the truth of who God is.

Focus Point

"For from the rising of the sun, even to its going down, My name shall be great among the Gentiles... My name shall be great among the nations," says the Lord of hosts. (Malachi 1:11, NKJV)

This verse unveils the heartbeat of God's plan: the exaltation of His name. When we recognize the greatness of His name, it stirs worship, repentance, and intercession. A low view of God leads to weak prayers. But when His greatness fills our vision, our voices cannot remain silent. He is not a distant deity; He is a glorious Father whose name will be worshiped in every nation. Seeing Him rightly transforms how we approach Him—and how we live.

Main Theme

The chapter emphasizes that prayer flows directly from our understanding of who God is. When our perception of God is rooted in lies—believing He's stingy, limited, or indifferent—our prayer lives become cold and lifeless. But when we see Him rightly—beautiful, merciful, powerful, near—prayer becomes joyful and faith-filled. Jesus modeled this in the Lord's Prayer by anchoring it in relationship: *"Our Father in heaven."* He invites us to rediscover the glory of God, not only in theological terms but through a personal encounter. The greatness of God's name is the foundation of intercession.

"The revelation of who God is transforms how we pray—and who we become."

Key Scriptures

- *"Our Father in heaven, hallowed be Your name."* (Matthew 6:9, NKJV)
- *"Who is like the Lord our God, Who dwells on high, Who humbles Himself to behold the things that are in the heavens and in the earth?"* (Psalm 113:5–6, NKJV)
- *"Blessed are you, Simon Bar-Jonah... and I also say to you that you are Peter... I will give you the keys of the kingdom of heaven."* (Matthew 16:17–19, NKJV)

Key Points

- **A Confronting Question** God asked me, "Who do you think you're talking to?" It was a holy reminder that prayer begins with beholding Him rightly.
- **Wrong Views of God Destroy Intimacy** When we believe lies about God's character, we lose the desire to pray. We must confront these lies and renew our minds with truth.
- **God Is Uncreated and Matchless** He is not like anyone else. He measures oceans in His palm and names every star. When we see His majesty, faith rises.
- **Jesus Is Beautiful Beyond Description** Revelation 1 and 4 reveal the glory of Jesus and the Father. His beauty, fire, mercy, and majesty are meant to fascinate our hearts.
- **Identity Is Found in Revelation** When Peter confessed Jesus' identity, Jesus revealed Peter's. Knowing who God is unlocks who we are.
- **We Pray with Authority When We Know Him** Jesus said the Church would have authority to bind and loose based on our revelation of Him. This is the foundation of victorious prayer.
- **God Delights in Us** Isaiah 62 reveals that knowing God delights in us gives us endurance in prayer. Intimacy fuels perseverance.

Journaling Questions

Journaling this chapter gives space for God to confront and heal the deepest misconceptions about Himself. Many believers have unknowingly projected past pain or cultural distortions onto God. Journaling is the tool that invites clarity. As you reflect on who you think God is, you'll uncover whether your theology aligns with truth—or with fear. Writing helps you process the lies, confess them, and replace them with Scripture-rooted revelation.

By engaging with this section, expect the Lord to gently reveal your personal view of Him. Do you see Him as generous or distant? Patient or disappointed? You may discover that the God you've prayed to is not the God revealed in Scripture. But don't be discouraged. This is the beginning of transformation. God wants you to see Him rightly so you can relate to Him deeply. These questions will help realign your heart and invite God into the core of your belief system.

Confronting the Lies

What misconceptions have I believed about God's nature that may be hindering my prayer life?

_____
_____
_____
_____
_____
_____
_____

Rediscovering God's Beauty

How does Revelation 4 or the description of Jesus in Revelation 1 change the way I view prayer?

_____
_____
_____
_____
_____
_____

God the Father, Not a Boss

Have I been talking to God as a loving Father or as a disappointed taskmaster?

_____
_____
_____
_____
_____
_____

My True Identity

Like Peter, have I allowed God to define who I am in light of who He is?

_____
_____
_____
_____
_____
_____

Confidence in His Delight

How would my prayer life change if I truly believed that God enjoys me and wants to hear my voice?

_____
_____
_____
_____
_____
_____

Actionable Steps

Cultivate a Daily Revelation of God
Spend 5 minutes each day meditating on a description of God from Scripture. Start with Psalm 113, Isaiah 40, or Revelation 4.

Equip Yourself by Studying God's Attributes
Make a list of God's attributes (love, mercy, justice, jealousy, etc.). For each, find one Scripture and write what it reveals about His nature.

Engage with God as a Father
Begin your prayers with "Father" and pause. Ask the Holy Spirit to show you what kind of Father He truly is. Let that guide your language.

Personal Reflection

As you reflect on the truths in this chapter, I want to ask you a sacred question: *Who do you think you're talking to?* The answer to that question will either fuel or frustrate your prayer life. If you believe God is distant or too busy, you'll shrink back. But if you believe He is majestic, generous, and full of love toward you, everything will change. Your voice will rise, not in religious duty, but in confidence. His throne will no longer feel far—it will feel like home.

You were made for intimacy with a glorious God. You were never meant to settle for a distant relationship built on duty. His eyes burn with love. His throne radiates beauty. And His ears are inclined toward you. As you rediscover His greatness and His delight in you, you'll find yourself praying—not because you have to—but because you're overwhelmed by who He is.

Do I believe God is truly as good as He says He is? Do I see myself the way He sees me? Am I willing to reject every lie and pursue the truth that transforms my prayer life?

_____
_____
_____
_____
_____
_____
_____
_____
_____
_____
_____
_____
_____
_____

Closing Prayer: *Father, forgive me for the times I have spoken to You through the filter of fear or lies. I renounce every distorted view I've held of You. I declare today that You are good, glorious, generous, and near. You are the Father who delights in me, the King who welcomes me, the God whose name is great. Fill my heart with a fresh revelation of who You are, and teach me to pray in awe, in truth, and in love. Amen.*

Chapter 3

What Do You Want, God?

"Now this is the confidence that we have in Him, that if we ask anything according to His will, He hears us." (1 John 5:14, NKJV)

I remember those early days when revival had just touched our community. I was barely twenty, freshly saved, and utterly undone by the presence of God. Every prayer meeting felt like standing at the edge of heaven. My closest companions were four older women who carried a mantle of intercession, and I clung to their every word. In those days, prayer wasn't a discipline—it was breath. I was hungry to see the Spirit poured out again, desperate to keep the fire of revival alive.

But when the revival waned and the meetings thinned, the silence felt suffocating. I couldn't accept that we would return to "normal." I tried to rouse the Church with exhortations, begged them to wake up, to pray, to care. But Monday prayer meetings were still nearly empty. The longer this went on, the more my heart grew bitter. I was crushed under the weight of disappointment, believing it was my responsibility to birth the next move of God.

It wasn't until I learned to ask a simple but life-altering question—*"What do You want, God?"*—that everything began to change. Intercession was never meant to begin with our will. It's not about persuading a reluctant God to move. It's about receiving His desires and then returning them to Him in prayer. I learned that prayer doesn't start with me. It starts with Him.

Many of us are praying from exhaustion because we've never paused to ask what God actually desires. But when we do, when we root our prayers in His will, our confidence is restored. We no longer strive—we partner. And that changes everything.

Focus Point

"Now this is the confidence that we have in Him, that if we ask anything according to His will, He hears us." (1 John 5:14, NKJV)

This verse is a declaration of divine alignment. Confidence in prayer is not a feeling—it is the fruit of agreement with God's will. We don't pray to impress God or to convince Him. We pray because He has revealed His heart. When we know what He wants, we can pray with boldness, authority, and peace. Prayer becomes a response, not a performance.

Main Theme

This chapter reveals that confidence in prayer is rooted in God's desires—not our own. When we pray according to His will, we partner with heaven and release His plans into the earth. Every major move of God, from Genesis to Revelation, flows from divine intention. Our role as intercessors is to discover what's on God's heart and echo it back to Him. Whether it's revival, healing, or the restoration of all things, prayer becomes powerful when it begins with the question: *"What do You want, God?"*

"Revival isn't our idea—it's His. And prayer is the invitation to agree with His heart."

Key Scriptures

- *"Now this is the confidence that we have in Him, that if we ask anything according to His will, He hears us."* (1 John 5:14, NKJV)
- *"Having made known to us the mystery of His will... that He might gather together in one all things in Christ, both which are in heaven and which are on earth—in Him."* (Ephesians 1:9–10, NKJV)
- *"Father, I desire that they also whom You gave Me may be with Me where I am, that they may behold My glory..."* (John 17:24, NKJV)

Key Points

- **Confidence Flows from Agreement** We don't pray with authority because of eloquence, but because we are aligned with God's will.
- **Prayer Begins with Receiving** Burnout happens when we initiate rather than respond. Intercession is about receiving His burden, not carrying our own.
- **God Desires Union** From the beginning, God's ultimate desire has been intimacy—He wants to dwell with us.
- **The Garden Was God's First Temple** God created Eden as a dwelling place to commune with man. His goal hasn't changed.
- **Separation Created the Need for Intercession** Sin caused a chasm between heaven and earth. Intercession is the bridge built by Christ and carried by His people.
- **The Entire Bible Tells a Story of Restoration** From Genesis to Revelation, the central narrative is God reconciling heaven and earth through Jesus.
- **We Are Invited to Partner in the Plan** God's will is not automatic—it requires intercessors to pray His purposes into fulfillment.

Journaling Questions

This chapter's journaling section invites readers into a deeper posture of listening. Most people approach prayer as a way to get God involved in their circumstances. But this chapter flips that paradigm, urging us to enter prayer by first asking: *God, what is on Your heart?* Through journaling, readers will begin to hear more clearly, aligning their prayers not with emotion or need, but with eternal purpose. Journaling becomes the sacred place where the heart of God is revealed.

As you answer the questions below, expect your prayer life to be reoriented. You will feel the difference between striving in prayer and flowing with God. As you hear His desire for union, for restoration, for revival, you'll realize that your groan echoes His. Journaling here is not only personal—it is prophetic. It marks your agreement with heaven.

Confessing Control

Have I tried to initiate revival, change, or breakthrough without first asking what God desires?

_____
_____
_____
_____
_____
_____
_____

Reorienting to Receive

What would it look like for me to receive God's burden in prayer instead of carrying my own?

_____
_____
_____
_____
_____
_____

The Story of Union

How have I seen the theme of intimacy and union with God in my own journey?

_____
_____
_____
_____
_____
_____

Agreeing with Restoration

Do I believe God wants to reconcile heaven and earth—and what is my part in that?

_____
_____
_____
_____
_____
_____

Confidence Reclaimed

How does knowing God wants these things more than I do change the way I pray?

_____
_____
_____
_____
_____
_____

Actionable Steps

Cultivate Listening Prayer
Begin each prayer time by asking, "God, what do You want today?" Then pause. Wait. Listen. Write what you hear.

Equip Yourself with His Promises
Study passages like Ephesians 1:9–10 and John 17:24. Write out what they say about God's desires. Let these shape your intercession.

Engage the Long Story
Reflect on the grand narrative of Scripture—from Eden to Revelation. Ask the Spirit to help you find your role in the restoration of all things.

Personal Reflection

If you're weary in prayer, it might be because you've carried burdens that God never asked you to bear. He's not calling you to manufacture revival or make His promises come true. He's inviting you into partnership—to listen, to agree, and to pray from His heart. The shift from performance to presence changes everything. Prayer becomes joy. Intercession becomes rest. Burdens become shared. You no longer pray to make something happen—you pray because God already has a plan.

You were created to stand in the gap—not in panic, but in purpose. There is confidence available to you, not because of your words, but because of His will. You don't need to twist His arm. You just need to ask what's on His heart—and echo it. Prayer is about God's desire for union, and you are part of that unfolding plan.

Am I praying from God's heart or from my own frustration? Do I trust that He longs for revival, healing, and union even more than I do? Am I ready to rest in His will and partner in His work?

Closing Prayer: *Father, I surrender every prayer I've prayed from striving and not from Your Spirit. Teach me to begin by listening. Reveal what's on Your heart and align my will with Yours. Thank You for the invitation to pray not from pressure, but from partnership. Let my voice echo the cry of heaven, and let my heart burn with the desire that burns in You—union with Your people. In Jesus' name, Amen.*

Chapter 4

The Revelation of Intercession

"Therefore He is also able to save to the uttermost those who come to God through Him, since He always lives to make intercession for them." (Hebrews 7:25, NKJV)

When I first heard the phrase *"He always lives to make intercession,"* something inside me shifted. It wasn't just a theological statement—it was a piercing revelation. Jesus, right now, is alive—not just as a memory or a Savior on a cross—but as an eternal Intercessor. He is not passive. He is not waiting. He is actively speaking, pleading, and releasing the will of the Father into the earth. And He invites us to join Him.

This chapter was born from that truth. We often talk about Jesus as our Savior, Redeemer, and King—and rightly so. But how often do we meditate on the fact that His current ministry is intercession? It's what He's doing right now. And if we are His body, then shouldn't we be doing what He's doing? Intercession is not an add-on for the spiritually elite; it is the heart of Jesus' present-day ministry and the call of every believer.

Once I saw Jesus as the eternal Intercessor, it reframed everything. Intercession wasn't just me praying to God—it was me joining with Jesus. It wasn't me trying to get heaven's attention —it was me echoing heaven's cry. Intercession became less about striving and more about communion. It became about agreeing with what Jesus is already praying.

What if we've made prayer harder than it has to be? What if intercession is simply agreeing with the heart of Jesus? If that's true, then intercession isn't just a task—it's the highest honor. We don't stand alone. We stand beside the risen Son of God, lifting our voice with His, shaping history with heaven's decree.

Focus Point

"Therefore He is also able to save to the uttermost those who come to God through Him, since He always lives to make intercession for them." (Hebrews 7:25, NKJV)

This verse is the clearest glimpse into the current ministry of Jesus. His work on the cross is finished, but His role as Intercessor continues. He is always interceding—unceasing, eternal, unstoppable. And His intercession isn't weak; it saves to the uttermost. When we intercede, we are not initiating—we are joining Him. Intercession, then, is not about performance but participation in His unending prayer.

Main Theme

The central theme of this chapter is that Jesus is our eternal Intercessor, and we are invited to partner with Him in the ministry of intercession. This revelation is not only theological—it is deeply personal. When we see Jesus in His current heavenly role, our own calling becomes clearer. Intercession is not just what we do; it's who we are becoming. The Spirit draws us into this priestly partnership so that we might become one with His voice and release His will into the earth.

"We are not just praying to Jesus—we are praying with Jesus."

Key Scriptures

- *"Therefore He is also able to save to the uttermost... since He always lives to make intercession for them."* (Hebrews 7:25, NKJV)
- *"Christ Jesus... is even at the right hand of God, who also makes intercession for us."* (Romans 8:34, NKJV)
- *"The Spirit Himself makes intercession for us with groanings which cannot be uttered."* (Romans 8:26, NKJV)

Key Points

- **Jesus Is Alive—and Interceding** His resurrection life is not passive. He is alive, at the right hand of the Father, making intercession on our behalf.
- **Intercession Is His Eternal Ministry** He's not just our past Savior—He's our present Intercessor. He ever lives to pray for us.
- **We Join His Intercession, Not Start Our Own** Prayer begins with listening. We're not initiating—we're agreeing with what He's already praying.
- **The Spirit Groans with Us and for Us** We are not alone in intercession. The Holy Spirit groans within us, aligning our hearts to God's will.
- **Intercession Releases Salvation and Transformation** He saves to the uttermost through intercession. Prayer is not just words—it's power that transforms.
- **Agreement Unlocks Heaven** When our hearts and mouths align with His voice, heaven's purposes are released on earth.
- **Prayer Is the Path to Intimacy and Authority** Intercession is not just impact—it's union. As we pray with Jesus, we become more like Him.

Journaling Questions

This chapter calls readers to rethink prayer entirely. Through journaling, readers can shift from viewing prayer as effort to seeing it as encounter. When we realize that Jesus is interceding, we learn to enter into His flow instead of forcing our own. Journaling here becomes a sacred space where we ask, "What are You praying, Jesus—and how can I agree?"

Expect God to speak as you write. Expect Him to reveal His groanings, His tears, His desires. You may feel the pull to intercede for people or places you've never thought about before. You may discover that your burdens are actually invitations from Jesus. This reflection isn't about perfection—it's about alignment. Let Him draw you into His prayer life.

Beholding the Intercessor

What does it mean to me personally that Jesus is always praying for me?

_____
_____
_____

Joining the Conversation

Have I ever asked Jesus what He is praying—and how I can partner with Him?

Holy Spirit Partnership

How have I experienced the Spirit groaning through me in prayer, even when I didn't have the words?

The Weight of Agreement

What would shift in my life if I prayed less from reaction and more from revelation?

Becoming Like Him

How is intercession shaping me into the image of Jesus?

_____
_____
_____
_____
_____
_____

Actionable Steps

Cultivate Spirit-Led Listening
Before praying for needs, ask Jesus, "What are You praying today?" Wait in stillness. Let Him speak.

Equip Yourself with Scriptural Intercession
Pray Hebrews 7:25 and Romans 8:34 aloud daily for a week. Declare His intercession over your life and others.

Engage in Prophetic Agreement
Write down the names of five people or situations. Ask Jesus what He is saying over them, and pray those words back to the Father.

Personal Reflection

Can you feel it? The invitation into deeper union, not just as a believer, but as a priest, a partner, a friend of Jesus. You were never meant to pray alone. The weight isn't on your shoulders. The outcome doesn't rely on your eloquence. Jesus is already praying. He is interceding with authority, with compassion, with unmatched power—and He's inviting you to join Him.

    This is more than prayer—it's identity. You were created to partner with the Intercessor. You were formed for this moment, to echo the sound of heaven, to release the purposes of God, to carry others before the throne with boldness. You don't need to know all the words—just bring your agreement. Just say yes.

Am I willing to slow down and ask Jesus what He's praying? Do I believe my voice carries power when it echoes His? Am I ready to align with heaven and become an intercessor in partnership with Christ?

Closing Prayer: *Jesus, I thank You that You are alive and interceding. You are not silent—you are speaking, pleading, and shaping history through Your prayers. Teach me to pray with You. Let my heart burn with what burns in Yours. Let my voice carry the sound of heaven. Holy Spirit, groan through me with prayers too deep for words. Make me one with Your intercession and use me to bring heaven to earth. In Jesus' name, Amen.*

Chapter 5

Old Testament Intercessors, Part 1

"So I sought for a man among them who would make a wall, and stand in the gap before Me on behalf of the land, that I should not destroy it; but I found no one." (Ezekiel 22:30, NKJV)

I remember the first time the Spirit of God gripped me with the lives of Old Testament intercessors. These weren't polished preachers or flawless heroes—they were broken, burning men and women who stood before God with trembling hearts and fierce devotion. When I studied the lives of Abraham, Moses, Samuel, and others, something ignited in me. They were more than Bible characters; they were mirrors—reflecting the kind of intimacy and authority we're all called to walk in.

In this chapter, we enter their stories—not as history lessons, but as divine invitations. God wasn't just recording facts—He was revealing a blueprint for partnership. He was showing us what it looks like when flawed humans carry divine burdens. These intercessors didn't simply ask for things; they contended, wept, wrestled, and pleaded with God until His mercy broke through judgment. They weren't casual in the prayer room. They were fiery, consistent, and often misunderstood. And yet, they moved the heart of God.

This chapter reminds us that God still searches for someone to stand in the gap. The call of Ezekiel 22:30 echoes through every generation: *"Who will intercede?"* The lives of these ancient intercessors weren't for their time alone—they are prophetic pictures of what's possible when one heart fully aligns with God's. The same Spirit that stirred them is stirring us.

Could it be that your breakthrough, your family's redemption, your city's awakening hinges on someone willing to stand in the gap? What if that someone is you?

Focus Point

"So I sought for a man among them who would make a wall, and stand in the gap before Me on behalf of the land... but I found no one." (Ezekiel 22:30, NKJV)

This verse is one of the most sobering in Scripture. God longed to show mercy, not judgment. He searched for an intercessor—someone to stand in the breach between a sinful people and a holy God. But none could be found. The implication is clear: prayer has power to stay judgment and release mercy. Intercessors are the difference between destruction and deliverance. God is still searching. Will He find you?

Main Theme

This chapter explores how the Old Testament intercessors operated as prototypes of New Testament prayer. From Abraham pleading for Sodom to Moses intervening on behalf of Israel, these stories show that intercession moves God's heart, even in the midst of judgment. God is not looking for perfection; He is looking for agreement. These intercessors teach us how to contend, how to stand in the gap, and how to carry God's burden with boldness.

"God is always searching for someone who will care enough to stand between heaven and earth."

Key Scriptures

- *"Then Abraham came near and said, 'Would You also destroy the righteous with the wicked?'"* (Genesis 18:23, NKJV)
- *"Yet now, if You will forgive their sin, but if not, I pray, blot me out of Your book which You have written."* (Exodus 32:32, NKJV)
- *"Moreover, as for me, far be it from me that I should sin against the Lord in ceasing to pray for you..."* (1 Samuel 12:23, NKJV)

Key Points

- **Abraham: The Friend Who Pleaded for Mercy** Abraham drew near to God on behalf of a wicked city. His intercession wasn't based on their worthiness—it was based on God's justice and mercy.
- **Moses: The Deliverer Who Stood in the Gap** After Israel sinned with the golden calf, Moses offered to be blotted out if God would spare them. His intercession came from deep love and holy fear.
- **Samuel: The Prophet Who Refused to Quit Praying** Even when Israel rejected God's leadership, Samuel declared that it would be a sin for him to stop praying. His commitment reveals the longevity of true intercession.
- **God Invites Human Partnership** Though He is sovereign, God chooses to act in partnership with intercessors. He honors their voices.
- **Intercession is Costly** These men carried the burden of others' failures. They were often misunderstood, rejected, or isolated—but they remained faithful.
- **Boldness and Brokenness Go Together** Old Testament intercessors were not arrogant. Their boldness came from knowing God's character. Their brokenness came from love for others.
- **God Still Seeks a Man** Ezekiel 22:30 is not a relic of the past—it is a cry for the present. God still looks for someone willing to stand in the gap.

Journaling Questions

Journaling after this chapter provides a chance to examine your own heart in light of the ancient intercessors. Their stories are not meant to inspire from a distance—they are meant to call us near. They challenge our comfort, confront our passivity, and invite us into God's aching heart for mercy. As you journal, expect God to highlight people, cities, or situations He's asking you to carry in prayer.

Don't rush this process. Write slowly. Let the Spirit search you. Let Him place His burden in your soul. Journaling here is an invitation to become part of a lineage of intercessors. It's where calling and compassion collide. It's where you say, "Here I am—send me to the secret place."

Examining the Wall

What "gaps" in my family, community, or nation is God asking me to stand in?

Learning from Abraham

How can I intercede for the lost without falling into judgment or bitterness?

Carrying the Burden

Am I willing to weep and contend for others like Moses, even if it costs me comfort?

Long-Term Intercession

Like Samuel, am I committed to praying for people—even when they reject God's leadership?

Becoming the One He Finds

If God is still searching for someone to stand in the gap, what's keeping me from saying yes?

Actionable Steps

Cultivate a Daily Burden
Ask God, "Who or what is on Your heart today?" Write it down. Carry it in prayer for 7 days.

Equip Yourself with Intercessor Stories
Reread Genesis 18 and Exodus 32 aloud. Let their boldness become your blueprint.

Engage with a Local Gap
Identify one place of injustice, spiritual dryness, or brokenness near you—and begin praying specifically for breakthrough.

Personal Reflection

You don't need a title, platform, or pulpit to shape history. You need a heart. A heart that breaks for what breaks His. A heart that stands when others flee. A heart that dares to believe prayer matters. That's what Abraham had. That's what Moses carried. That's what Samuel lived. And that's what God is looking for in you.

There are gaps in the wall. Gaps in cities, in schools, in families, in churches. The storm is real. The breach is wide. But you are not powerless. You are not unqualified. You are not too late. Heaven is still looking for someone. Someone who will say, "God, I'll stand there. I'll carry them. I'll cry out until mercy breaks through."

Am I willing to stand between judgment and mercy? Am I ready to carry others before God even when they cannot pray for themselves? Will I be the one God finds when He looks for an intercessor?

Closing Prayer: *Father, I say yes. I will stand in the gap. I will not wait for someone else. Make me bold like Abraham, burdened like Moses, and faithful like Samuel. Teach me to contend for mercy when judgment seems inevitable. Use my voice to stay destruction and release Your kindness. Let me be the one You find when You search the earth. In Jesus' name, Amen.*

Chapter 6

Old Testament Intercessors, Part 2

"But truly, as I live, all the earth shall be filled with the glory of the Lord... I will pardon according to your word." (Numbers 14:21, 20, NKJV)

There's a story that has marked my life—a moment in Scripture where a man's voice moved the heart of God and altered the fate of a nation. In Numbers 14, after Israel rebelled and refused to enter the Promised Land, God declared judgment. But then Moses stepped in. He didn't plead based on Israel's righteousness. He didn't shift blame or make excuses. He simply reminded God of His own glory and mercy. And God said, *"I have pardoned according to your word."* That verse stuns me every time. God didn't pardon because the people repented—He pardoned because a man stood in the gap.

In this chapter, we continue exploring the intercessors of the Old Testament. These weren't casual prayers—they were cries from men like Moses, David, Elijah, and Daniel—people who carried both fire and tears in their souls. They spoke God's language. They wept with His compassion. And they stood boldly when others shrank back.

This chapter reveals that God's pattern hasn't changed. He still responds to intercessors. He still moves when someone stands between mercy and judgment. These stories aren't relics—they're roadmaps. And the invitation is still open: *"Will you be one of them?"*

What would happen if you believed your words could shift a nation's destiny? What if your intercession was the hinge point for someone else's breakthrough?

Focus Point

"But truly, as I live, all the earth shall be filled with the glory of the Lord... I have pardoned according to your word." (Numbers 14:21, 20, NKJV)

This is one of the clearest displays of God responding directly to a man's intercession. Even in the face of rebellion and judgment, God pauses and says, "Because of your prayer, I will show mercy." This verse reveals both God's desire to fill the earth with His glory and His willingness to partner with intercessors to release it. Our words matter. Our alignment matters. Heaven still listens.

Main Theme

This chapter highlights how the prayers of intercessors in the Old Testament repeatedly stayed the hand of judgment, released revival, and prepared the way for God's purposes. Intercession was never secondary in Scripture—it was central. Men like Moses, David, Elijah, and Daniel demonstrate that one person aligned with heaven can change the course of history. God is not looking for mass appeal—He's looking for agreement.

"God listens when His friends speak."

Key Scriptures

- *"Pardon the iniquity of this people, I pray, according to the greatness of Your mercy... Then the Lord said: 'I have pardoned, according to your word.'"* (Numbers 14:19–20, NKJV)
- *"When David saw the angel... he said, 'Surely I have sinned... but these sheep, what have they done?'"* (2 Samuel 24:17, NKJV)
- *"While I was speaking, praying, and confessing... yes, while I was speaking in prayer, the man Gabriel... reached me..."* (Daniel 9:20–21, NKJV)

Key Points

- **Moses: Interceding with God's Glory in Mind** He appealed not to Israel's goodness, but to God's mercy and reputation among the nations.
- **David: Brokenness Births True Intercession** When he saw judgment coming, David took full responsibility and cried out for the people's sake.
- **Elijah: Boldness and Fire** He called down fire and ended a drought with one prayer—because he prayed with heaven's authority.
- **Daniel: Identifying with a Nation's Sin** He repented on behalf of others, standing as if the guilt were his own. His humility moved angels.
- **God Responds to the Voice of One** Each of these men stood largely alone. But God responded because of their alignment and surrender.
- **Intercession Is Both Bold and Broken** True intercession carries both courage and compassion. It's not demanding—it's deeply surrendered.
- **You're Invited into the Same Story** These are not "Bible-only" callings. Their stories are patterns for every believer filled with God's Spirit.

Journaling Questions

Journaling in this chapter takes you into the posture of the intercessors. This isn't about admiring them—it's about becoming one. These men carried the burden of generations, and God moved because of their yieldedness. Journaling invites you to ask hard questions: Where do I need to own my city's brokenness? Who do I need to weep over? Am I willing to be the one?

This reflection will help you move from passive observation to prophetic partnership. Write with openness. Let the stories of Moses, David, Elijah, and Daniel challenge your view of intercession. Let their tears become your invitation.

When Mercy Overrules Judgment

Have I ever seen God show mercy in response to my prayers for others?

_____
_____
_____

Taking Responsibility Like David

Where is God asking me to intercede, not from blame, but from broken identification?

_____
_____
_____
_____
_____
_____

Elijah's Boldness

Am I afraid to pray big prayers because I fear they won't happen? What does bold intercession look like in my life?

_____
_____
_____
_____
_____
_____

Daniel's Humility

What does it mean to repent on behalf of others, even when I didn't commit the sin?

_____
_____
_____
_____
_____
_____

Pardoned According to My Word

Do I believe that my words, aligned with God, can change circumstances, cities, or nations?

_____
_____
_____
_____
_____
_____

Actionable Steps

Cultivate Consistent Intercession
Choose one area of injustice, spiritual need, or national crisis—and pray over it daily for the next 30 days.

Equip Yourself with Biblical Blueprints
Study the prayers of Moses (Numbers 14), Daniel (Daniel 9), and Elijah (1 Kings 18). Let their language inform your own.

Engage in Repentance for Others
Write a prayer of confession on behalf of your city, your church, or your family—modeling Daniel 9.

Personal Reflection

God is not distant. He listens. And He moves in response to prayer. That truth humbles me and calls me higher. When I read that God pardoned a nation because of Moses' words... I realize: this is serious. This is not symbolic. It is reality. And it is happening now.

The earth is still groaning. Judgment still hangs over nations. Families still live in rebellion. But God is still asking, "Is there one who will pray?" Your voice matters more than you know. Heaven responds to friends who know the heart of the King.

Do I believe God still moves at the sound of intercession? Am I willing to carry another's burden before the throne? Will I be one of those whose words shift history because they are aligned with heaven?

Closing Prayer: *Lord, I thank You for the witness of Moses, David, Elijah, and Daniel. I thank You that You move when people pray. I ask You to make me one of them—an intercessor who stands between the people and Your purposes. Break my heart for what breaks Yours. Teach me how to cry out with fire and with tears. Let my words be shaped by Your Spirit, and let mercy flow because I prayed. In Jesus' name, Amen.*

Chapter 7

Jesus—His Intercession and Our Union with Him

"Therefore He is also able to save to the uttermost those who come to God through Him, since He always lives to make intercession for them." (Hebrews 7:25, NKJV)

I will never forget the first time I realized that Jesus was praying for me. Not just that He had prayed while on earth, but that even now—this very moment—He is interceding for me. That truth didn't just comfort me; it shook me. In a moment when I felt weak, overwhelmed by failure, and unsure of my future, the Holy Spirit whispered, *"Jesus is praying for you."* Everything changed. Suddenly, I wasn't alone. I wasn't forgotten. I was being carried in the prayers of the Son of God.

In this chapter, we move from studying intercessors to beholding *The Intercessor*. Jesus is not merely a historical figure who taught about prayer—He is currently, actively interceding. He stood in the gap on the cross, and now He stands before the Father as our Advocate and High Priest. He is the bridge, the intercessor, the eternal mediator between God and man. His intercession is not reactive; it is redemptive. It is not limited by time or space. He forever lives to intercede.

But here is the most breathtaking truth: He invites us into union with Him in that very ministry. Through the Spirit, we are not just saved by Jesus—we are joined to His present-day intercession. That means prayer is not something we initiate alone. We are stepping into a conversation that Jesus already began. Intercession is not our idea. It's His. And we are invited to participate.

Have you ever considered what it means that Jesus, even now, is praying for you? What would change if you lived from that reality?

Focus Point

"Therefore He is also able to save to the uttermost those who come to God through Him, since He always lives to make intercession for them." (Hebrews 7:25, NKJV)

This verse reveals the eternal and unchanging ministry of Jesus. His intercession didn't end at the cross or with the resurrection. He is alive—and He is praying. He intercedes not occasionally, but continually. This is how He saves us "to the uttermost"—not just forgiving our past, but sustaining our present and securing our future. His prayers never fail, and we are upheld by them.

Main Theme

Jesus is not only our Savior and Lord—He is our Eternal Intercessor. He stands before the Father on our behalf, carrying our names, our struggles, and our destiny in His prayers. His intercession is based on His finished work, His perfect obedience, and His unbreakable love. This chapter invites us to see prayer not just as a duty but as participation in Jesus' own heavenly ministry.

"Jesus is praying for you—and He invites you to pray with Him."

Key Scriptures

- *"It is Christ who died, and furthermore is also risen, who is even at the right hand of God, who also makes intercession for us."* (Romans 8:34, NKJV)
- *"I do not pray for these alone, but also for those who will believe in Me through their word."* (John 17:20, NKJV)
- *"And the Lord said, 'Simon, Simon! Indeed, Satan has asked for you... but I have prayed for you, that your faith should not fail.'"* (Luke 22:31-32, NKJV)

Key Points

- **Jesus Lives to Intercede** His current ministry is intercession. He is not passive in heaven—He is engaged in prayer.
- **His Intercession is Personal** Jesus does not pray in generalities. He names you. He sees your need and carries it to the Father.
- **Our Salvation is Sustained by His Prayers** Hebrews 7:25 declares He is able to save "to the uttermost" because He continues to pray for us.
- **We Are Joined to His Intercession** Through the Holy Spirit, we don't initiate prayer alone—we are joining in what Jesus is already praying.
- **Union Precedes Intercession** You must first see yourself as united with Christ before you can truly partner with Him in prayer.
- **Jesus Interceded Before the Cross** John 17 is a glimpse into the heart of Jesus. He prayed for unity, for protection, for glory—and He still prays these things.
- **Your Weakness is Covered by His Strength** When Satan desired to sift Peter, Jesus didn't rebuke Peter—He prayed for him. That's how He treats us, too.

Journaling Questions

Journaling after this chapter is a sacred opportunity to step into the reality of being prayed for by Jesus. Let that sink in. You are not alone. Jesus knows your weakness. He has prayed for your faith not to fail. Journaling will help you meditate on the ways Jesus has carried you, especially when you didn't even know it.

These journal questions are not abstract—they are meant to open your heart to the presence of the Intercessor. As you reflect, let the reality of His prayers for you lead you to greater trust, boldness, and intimacy. You are not trying to earn His attention. You already have it.

Jesus is Praying Right Now

What does it mean to me that Jesus is actively praying for me at this moment?

_____
_____
_____
_____

Union in Intercession

How can I join Jesus in what He's already praying, instead of trying to start on my own?

_____
_____
_____
_____
_____
_____

When I Couldn't Pray

Can I remember a time when I felt carried, even though I wasn't praying? Could that have been Jesus interceding?

_____
_____
_____
_____
_____
_____

Jesus and Peter

How has Jesus' intercession preserved me, like it did for Peter, when I faced spiritual attack or failure?

_____
_____
_____
_____
_____
_____

A Life of Agreement

What areas of my life need to come into agreement with Jesus' intercession right now?

_____
_____
_____
_____
_____

Actionable Steps

Cultivate Awareness of His Intercession
Each morning this week, pause and say: "Jesus, I thank You that You are praying for me right now." Let it shape your mindset.

Equip Your Spirit with the Word
Read John 17 slowly and aloud. Let the prayers of Jesus become the framework for your own.

Engage in Intercession with Jesus
Ask the Holy Spirit, "What is Jesus praying today?" Wait in stillness. Write what comes, and begin to pray in agreement.

Personal Reflection

This chapter is one of the most sacred truths I've ever encountered: Jesus prays for me. He doesn't condemn me when I fail. He prays. He doesn't abandon me when I'm confused. He intercedes. That revelation has become an anchor in every storm. No matter how I feel, no matter what I face—He is speaking my name before the Father.

And now, as one joined to Him, I get to speak with Him. Not just to Him. I get to echo His prayers. I get to weep where He weeps, to plead where He pleads, and to rejoice where He rejoices. Intercession is no longer burdensome. It's a union. And it's beautiful.

Do I live as someone who is prayed for by Jesus? Am I listening for what He's saying from the throne? Am I ready to partner with my Intercessor in prayer that touches the heart of God and changes the world?

Closing Prayer: *Jesus, thank You that You never stop praying for me. When I stumble, You pray. When I'm weak, You intercede. I receive the strength of Your prayers today. Help me to live with awareness of Your intercession and to join You in it. Teach me to pray not from striving, but from union. Let my heart burn with what burns in Yours. Amen.*

Chapter 8

Teach Us to Pray

"Now it came to pass, as He was praying in a certain place, when He ceased, that one of His disciples said to Him, 'Lord, teach us to pray, as John also taught his disciples.'" (Luke 11:1, NKJV)

There's something striking about this scene in the Gospel of Luke. The disciples had seen Jesus perform miracles, preach to multitudes, and walk on water. But they never asked, *"Teach us to heal,"* or *"Teach us to preach."* They asked, *"Teach us to pray."* That tells us something about what impacted them the most. They saw something in Jesus' private prayer life that left them hungry. They heard the tone of His voice, witnessed the intimacy He had with the Father, and realized this was the secret to everything.

I've often said that we need more than sermons—we need groaning. We need that place where words give way to hunger, where prayer is not polished but raw, where we stop performing and start communing. This chapter is a cry for that kind of prayer life—not learned from textbooks but from being near Jesus. Prayer is not a formula to master; it's a Person to encounter. The disciples saw that prayer wasn't what Jesus did. It was who He was.

When we say, "Teach us to pray," we're not just asking for instructions. We're asking for impartation. We're asking to be drawn into that sacred rhythm of communion that defined Jesus' life. He didn't pray because He had to. He prayed because He *loved* to. And when we ask Him to teach us, we're asking to love the Father like He does, to depend like He did, and to be shaped into the kind of people who carry heaven's heartbeat.

What if our greatest spiritual growth began not with more knowledge, but with a deeper hunger to learn how to talk to God like Jesus did?

Focus Point

"Now it came to pass, as He was praying in a certain place, when He ceased, that one of His disciples said to Him, 'Lord, teach us to pray...'" (Luke 11:1, NKJV)

This verse captures the longing that every disciple of Jesus must carry. It reveals that prayer is something to be learned, but more importantly, it is something to be caught by proximity. The disciples didn't learn prayer through information—they learned it by watching intimacy. Jesus' prayer life was so compelling, so real, and so consuming that it ignited hunger in those who observed Him. This is the cry of a true disciple: "Teach me to pray like You do."

Main Theme

The heart of this chapter is the burning desire to be taught by Jesus how to pray. It is an acknowledgment that true prayer cannot be faked or forced—it must be forged through relationship. The disciples saw something in Jesus' secret life that surpassed public miracles. They witnessed communion. The chapter reminds us that prayer isn't simply a discipline; it's a desire to know God. And that desire, when nurtured, gives birth to powerful, heaven-moving intercession.

"The greatest prayer you'll ever pray may simply be: 'Lord, teach me to pray.'"

Key Scriptures

- *"Lord, teach us to pray, as John also taught his disciples."* (Luke 11:1, NKJV)
- *"He went out to the mountain to pray, and continued all night in prayer to God."* (Luke 6:12, NKJV)
- *"In the morning, having risen a long while before daylight, He went out and departed to a solitary place; and there He prayed."* (Mark 1:35, NKJV)

Key Points

- **Prayer is Taught in the Secret Place** The disciples learned prayer not through a class, but by watching Jesus commune with the Father.

- **Prayer is Caught, Not Just Taught** It's not only about words—it's about the spirit behind the words. Hunger is more powerful than technique.
- **Jesus Modeled Relational Prayer** He prayed often, passionately, and alone. His prayer life wasn't routine—it was intimacy.
- **Teachability is the Starting Point** The request "Teach us to pray" reveals humility and hunger. We must approach prayer as students.
- **Consistency Fuels Power** Jesus prayed early, late, and long. His consistency was a reflection of dependence.
- **Prayer is a Foundation, Not an Accessory** Jesus didn't fit prayer into His life. His life flowed from prayer.
- **We Must Return to the Simplicity of Asking** Sometimes the most powerful prayer is simply, "Lord, I don't know how. Teach me."

Journaling Questions

This chapter's journaling section calls you to go deeper than technique—it invites you into intimacy. "Teach us to pray" is not just a question. It's a confession that we don't know how to reach God on our own. It's the beginning of a lifelong journey. Journaling here allows you to examine your current view of prayer and invite the Holy Spirit to reshape it.

Use these reflections to stir up hunger—not guilt. Jesus is not looking for perfect prayers. He's looking for surrendered hearts. Let this be the chapter where your desire to know God deepens, where you bring your questions and walk away with impartation. Write honestly. Ask boldly. Listen closely.

The Cry of a Disciple

Have I ever truly asked Jesus to teach me to pray? What would change if I did?

_____
_____
_____
_____
_____
_____
_____

Learning by Watching

Who in my life models the kind of prayer life that stirs hunger in me?

My Current Prayer Posture

What do my current habits of prayer reveal about my relationship with God?

Prayer as Priority

How can I shift prayer from being a duty to being the source of my life?

Returning to Simplicity

What's one simple step I can take to pray more like Jesus?

_____
_____
_____
_____
_____

Actionable Steps

Cultivate a Teachable Spirit
Begin every prayer time this week by saying, "Lord, teach me to pray." Let Him lead the conversation.

Equip Your Mind with the Gospels
Spend the next seven days reading a different passage where Jesus prayed (e.g., Luke 6:12, Mark 1:35). Take notes on how He prayed.

Engage in Imitation Before Innovation
Rather than trying to create your own style, begin by mimicking Jesus' posture: early, alone, dependent, consistent.

Personal Reflection

This chapter draws me back to the simplicity of childlike hunger. I don't need to impress God with lofty words. I need to ask for help. I need to return to that posture where my soul whispers, "Lord, teach me." There is no shame in that question. There is power in it. When we stop pretending to have it all together, we finally become students—and students get filled.

I'm encouraged by the thought that Jesus *wants* to teach me. He's not frustrated with my weakness. He's not looking for experts—He's looking for followers. And prayer is the pathway where followers become friends, and friends become lovers of God.

Am I willing to admit I still need to be taught? Will I let Jesus take the lead in my prayer life?

Am I hungry enough to ask, wait, and listen as He teaches me to pray from His heart, not just my need?

Closing Prayer: *Lord Jesus, thank You for being the Master of prayer and the Teacher of those who hunger. I ask You today to teach me to pray. Not as a ritual or duty, but as a rhythm of love. Draw me into the kind of communion You shared with the Father. Let my prayers be marked by hunger, not habit. Form me in the secret place until I pray like You. Amen.*

Chapter 9

The Furnace of Prayer

"Rejoicing in hope, patient in tribulation, continuing steadfastly in prayer." (Romans 12:12, NKJV)

The furnace marked me. I remember walking into the prayer room on the brink of burnout—physically tired, emotionally spent, spiritually confused. But something pulled me in. I saw others in that room, not doing ministry, not striving to be seen, but simply burning. I watched lives be set on fire through steady, hidden prayer. That room became my furnace, and I've never been the same. It was there I discovered that God does His deepest work in secret places of heat, pressure, and sustained intimacy.

When we talk about prayer, we must move beyond casual conversation. The prayer room isn't a lounge—it's a furnace. A place of refining, purifying, transforming fire. This is where God reshapes hearts and reclaims souls. The prayer furnace is not for the faint of heart, but for the hungry. It's not about perfect words, but about surrendered lives. When we step into the fire of God's presence, we don't just offer prayers—we become offerings.

In this chapter, we return to the reality that sustained, burning prayer is not just for the spiritually elite. It is the birthplace of revival. God is not looking for more events—He's looking for furnaces. He's looking for people who will lay down their lives, who will persevere when it's hard, who will weep and rejoice in the secret place until heaven invades earth. The furnace is where eternal things are birthed.

Are you willing to enter the furnace—not for comfort, but for consecration?

Focus Point

"Rejoicing in hope, patient in tribulation, continuing steadfastly in prayer." (Romans 12:12, NKJV)

This verse beautifully outlines the rhythm of a burning heart: joy in hope, endurance in trials, and constancy in prayer. The furnace of prayer doesn't remove hardship—it produces endurance in the middle of it. It refines our desires, strengthens our faith, and anchors our hope. Paul understood this: that fervent, enduring prayer is the heartbeat of a life yielded to God.

Main Theme

This chapter challenges the reader to see prayer not as convenience, but as consecration. Prayer is not merely a quiet time—it is a burning time. The furnace is the place of ongoing transformation, where persistence births power, and where pain produces fire. Revival doesn't start in pulpits—it starts in prayer rooms. The furnace is not glamorous, but it is glorious. It's where God shapes history through hidden lives.

"God doesn't use microwaves—He uses furnaces."

Key Scriptures

- *"Never be lacking in zeal, but keep your spiritual fervor, serving the Lord."* (Romans 12:11, NIV)
- *"The fire shall ever be burning upon the altar; it shall never go out."* (Leviticus 6:13, KJV)
- *"Then one of the seraphim flew to me, having in his hand a live coal which he had taken with the tongs from the altar."* (Isaiah 6:6, NKJV)

Key Points

- **The Furnace Is Where Fire Is Sustained** The prayer room is the altar where the fire must never go out. It requires intentionality and consistency.
- **Prayer Is Painful Before It's Powerful** You'll often sweat and weep before you shout and win. Transformation begins in travail.
- **The Hidden Place Precedes the Public Move** Revival always starts in obscurity. God uses secret fires to birth public flames.
- **The Furnace Forms You** Before God sends you, He sets you apart. The furnace shapes identity and character.
- **We Must Persevere in Prayer** When prayer feels dry or fruitless, that's often where God is doing His deepest work.
- **The Fire Burns Away the Flesh** Selfish ambition and carnal distraction are consumed in sustained presence.
- **The Furnace Attracts Heaven** Wherever God finds fire, He sends His glory. Isaiah encountered angels in the fire.

Journaling Questions

This chapter's journaling experience will lead you into the heat of God's refining presence. The furnace is not a place of fear, but of formation. It is where we go when we're tired of shallow prayers and ready for real surrender. These reflections are designed to help you evaluate your current "furnace life"—and to invite you to stoke the flame.

Many run from the fire, but God invites you into it. Not to be burned up in destruction, but to be ignited for purpose. Prayer that costs nothing changes nothing. But prayer that persists through the furnace changes history. Let these journal questions call you deeper, beyond comfort into consecration.

My Furnace Experience

Have I ever entered into a season of sustained, hidden prayer that felt like a furnace? What did God refine in me?

_____
_____
_____
_____
_____
_____
_____

Enduring the Heat

What keeps me from persevering in prayer when it feels dry or difficult?

_____
_____
_____
_____
_____
_____

Offering Myself as Fuel

What areas of my life need to be laid on the altar as fuel for the fire?

_____
_____
_____
_____
_____
_____

Fire vs. Convenience

Am I more drawn to comfort or consecration in my relationship with God?

_____
_____
_____
_____
_____
_____

Becoming a Burning One

What would it look like for me to live as a prayer furnace that never goes out?

_____
_____
_____
_____
_____
_____

Actionable Steps

Cultivate a Daily Burning Place
Choose a set time and space each day this week where you meet God—not casually, but with the intention to burn.

Equip the Altar with Sacrifice
Offer something costly this week—your time, your entertainment, your comfort—as a living sacrifice in prayer.

Engage in a Furnace Fast
Take a day to fast and pray, asking God to ignite fresh fire. Let hunger rise as you wait on Him.

Personal Reflection

This chapter wrecks me every time. I remember what it felt like to be in that prayer room when nobody saw, and yet I knew God was watching. The furnace stripped away my pride, my performance, and my need for applause. And in the fire, I found freedom. There's something about the heat of God's presence that burns away everything false.

I don't want to be known for platform moments. I want to be known in heaven's furnace. I want to be one of those who burns, even when no one is watching. That's what this is about. Not chasing the spotlight, but living lit—alive with holy fire. That's what the world is longing to see: people who have been with God in the furnace.

Will I run into the fire or away from it? Will I let the furnace refine me or resist the pressure? Will I become the kind of intercessor who burns in secret so that heaven can move in public?

Closing Prayer: *Lord, ignite me in the furnace of prayer. I lay my life on Your altar today. Consume what is not of You, and set me ablaze with what pleases You. Teach me to persevere, to burn without burnout, to love the secret place more than the stage. I want to be a living offering, burning until You come. Amen.*

Chapter 10

Birthing Revival

"Before she was in labor, she gave birth; before her pain came, she delivered a male child. Who has heard such a thing? Who has seen such things? Shall the earth be made to give birth in one day? Or shall a nation be born at once? For as soon as Zion was in labor, she gave birth to her children."
(Isaiah 66:7–8, NKJV)

I'll never forget the moment I stepped into a prayer room where groans were rising. These weren't polished prayers. These were deep, raw, and desperate cries erupting from the hearts of intercessors. It wasn't just a room—it felt like a delivery room in the Spirit. I had read about revival, preached about it, even longed for it. But this was different. This was travail. This was birthing. The groans told me that heaven was about to release something—something costly, something holy.

Revival is not merely a series of meetings, signs, or wonders. Revival is the manifestation of God's presence breaking into time, space, and human hearts. And every true revival in history has been birthed in the furnace of intercession. You don't get revival by organizing better services—you get it by hosting God's presence. And hosting requires hunger, travail, and spiritual labor.

There is a sound in the Spirit—a groaning, a weeping, a contending—that comes from those who have felt the ache of what is not yet, but must be. It's the sound of a people who have seen a glimpse of what heaven wants to do and won't stop crying out until it breaks through. Birthing revival means carrying something that isn't for you alone—it's for nations, generations, and the glory of God.

Are you willing to groan so others can live? Are you ready to become the delivery room of God's dreams?

Focus Point

"As soon as Zion was in labor, she gave birth to her children." (Isaiah 66:8, NKJV)

This verse unveils the supernatural nature of spiritual birth. Zion, the representation of God's people, enters into labor, and immediately children are born. This is not a natural sequence—it's divine. Spiritual labor is not wasted. The groans of intercession are not empty. They produce birth, life, and legacy. What God wants to do in the earth hinges upon a people willing to labor until delivery comes.

Main Theme

This chapter calls us to embrace the role of spiritual midwives—those who posture themselves in the place of intercession until revival is born. Every move of God requires groaners before it welcomes gatherers. The groaning place is the birthing place. Like Elijah bowed on Mount Carmel or Hannah weeping in the temple, revival begins with those who will not be silent until heaven responds. If you want revival, you must be willing to birth it.

"Revival isn't shipped in from heaven—it's born through travail."

Key Scriptures

- *"And Elijah went up to the top of Carmel; then he bowed down on the ground, and put his face between his knees."* (1 Kings 18:42, NKJV)
- *"And being in agony, He prayed more earnestly. Then His sweat became like great drops of blood falling down to the ground."* (Luke 22:44, NKJV)
- *"My little children, for whom I labor in birth again until Christ is formed in you."* (Galatians 4:19, NKJV)

Key Points

- **Revival Requires Travailing Prayer** No lasting move of God is born without labor. Groaning in prayer precedes glory in power.
- **The Church Must Become the Delivery Room** We are not called to comfort but to childbirth—spiritual birth that brings heaven to earth.
- **Elijah Modeled Birthing Revival** He didn't just pray; he postured himself in labor. He travailed until the cloud appeared.
- **Jesus Groaned for Our Redemption** In Gethsemane, Jesus birthed the new covenant through blood, sweat, and surrender.
- **Revival Starts in the Secret Place** Before the crowds come, the cries must rise. The hidden laborers prepare the harvest.
- **You Carry Nations Inside You** Like Zion, you may not even realize what you're pregnant with until the labor begins.
- **Birth Is Painful but Worth It** The pain of prayer is nothing compared to the joy of what's produced through it.

Journaling Questions

This journaling section is a holy invitation. It's not a call to duty, but to divine partnership. You are being invited to carry something that matters—to groan for revival, to weep for the lost, to birth something heaven is waiting to release through you. These reflections will challenge your comfort, but they'll awaken your calling.

Let God speak to you here. He's not looking for impressive prayers; He's looking for surrendered wombs. Journal your surrender. Write your yes. Wrestle with your fears. And most of all, ask God to show you what He's trying to birth through your life.

My Spiritual Pregnancy

What do I believe God has placed inside me that needs to be birthed in this season?

_____
_____
_____
_____

Embracing the Labor

Am I willing to contend in prayer even when nothing seems to be happening?

_____
_____
_____
_____
_____
_____

The Cost of Revival

What comforts or routines must I release to make space for sustained intercession?

_____
_____
_____
_____
_____
_____

Becoming a Midwife for Others

Who am I called to intercede for until Christ is formed in them?

_____
_____
_____
_____
_____
_____

Carrying the Groan

What breaks my heart in prayer? What makes me groan beyond words?

_____
_____
_____
_____
_____
_____

Actionable Steps

Cultivate a Lifestyle of Travail
Set aside extended time each week to cry out for revival in your city, church, or nation. Let your heart break until His presence comes.

Equip Yourself with Testimonies of Revival
Read about past moves of God—like the Welsh Revival or Azusa Street—to fuel your intercession with vision.

Engage with a Prayer Group
Join or start a group committed to praying specifically for revival. Consistent, collective groaning multiplies the breakthrough.

Personal Reflection

This chapter stirs a cry inside me that I can't ignore. I realize now that revival doesn't come from platforms but from prayer closets. I'm not waiting for God to do something—He's waiting on me to labor with Him. The birth of revival depends on the faithfulness of those willing to stay in the labor room when others have left.

I don't want to spectate revival. I want to birth it. I want to groan until something holy breaks open over my generation. I know it will cost me comfort, predictability, and sometimes even relationships. But nothing compares to the joy of seeing spiritual life emerge where there was once barrenness.

Will I accept the call to carry what heaven is waiting to birth? Will I groan even when there's no sign of rain? Will I stay in the labor room until revival breaks through me and spills into the world around me?

Closing Prayer: *Lord, I surrender to Your purposes. Teach me to groan until something eternal is birthed through my life. Remove apathy, pride, and distraction. Make me a delivery room for revival. Let my heart break with what breaks Yours, and let my prayers rise like incense until the heavens open. I say yes to labor. I say yes to the groan. Use me to birth Your glory. Amen.*

Chapter 11

Where Is This Going?

"For the earth will be filled with the knowledge of the glory of the Lord, as the waters cover the sea."
(Habakkuk 2:14, NKJV)

There was a moment in the early days of the International House of Prayer when we were just a small community of burning hearts, praying day and night with barely a crowd. No cameras. No fame. Just the ache. I remember asking myself in those early, hidden years, "Where is this going?" We were giving ourselves to something with no blueprint, no payoff in sight. But God knew. He was planting seeds that would fill the earth with His glory. And now, decades later, we've only seen the beginning.

It's easy to lose sight of the bigger picture when you're knee-deep in the daily grind of prayer, fasting, and obedience. We often reduce the calling to our current assignment. But God is writing a larger story—a global narrative of revival, justice, and the return of His Son. He's not merely calling us to intercede; He's calling us to align our hearts with His eternal purpose. What you're doing in secret is connected to the fulfillment of God's promises over nations.

When we look at the Bible, we see a consistent theme: God's glory filling the earth, Jesus reigning from Jerusalem, and every tribe and tongue worshiping the Lamb. The culmination of history isn't chaos—it's glory. The end of your obedience isn't burnout—it's breakthrough. And though we may not always see the full picture, God sees it all. He knows what every "yes" to prayer, every act of faithfulness, every tear sown in intercession is producing in the unseen realm.

So, where is this going? It's going toward global glory. Toward revival. Toward Jesus receiving the reward of His suffering. The question is—are you willing to stay faithful even when the destination seems far?

Focus Point

"For the earth will be filled with the knowledge of the glory of the Lord, as the waters cover the sea." (Habakkuk 2:14, NKJV)

This verse captures the prophetic certainty of God's plan. The earth will—not might—be filled with His glory. This is the anchor for every intercessor and burning one. No matter what's happening politically, culturally, or personally, we labor under a guaranteed outcome. His glory will cover every place, and our prayers help prepare the way.

Main Theme

The ultimate goal of intercession and intimacy is not personal satisfaction, but global transformation. This chapter reminds us that all our prayers, groans, and sacrifices are moving history toward a climactic conclusion—Jesus reigning on the earth, His glory flooding the nations, and justice being established forever. Every hidden act of obedience is unto something eternal. We're not wasting our lives—we're investing them into a divine narrative that ends in glory.

"Your secret yes is filling the earth with glory."

Key Scriptures

- *"And the Spirit and the bride say, 'Come!' And let him who hears say, 'Come!'"* (Revelation 22:17, NKJV)
- *"Of the increase of His government and peace there will be no end."* (Isaiah 9:7, NKJV)
- *"Let Your kingdom come. Your will be done on earth as it is in heaven."* (Matthew 6:10, NKJV)

Key Points

- **God Has an Endgame** Every part of history is moving toward the fullness of God's kingdom on earth.
- **Your Obedience Fuels Eternity** Nothing done in secret is wasted. Every tear, every prayer is recorded in heaven.
- **We Are Preparing the Earth for Glory** Like John the Baptist, our intercession makes a highway for the King.
- **The Bride Must Be Made Ready** The Church is not just waiting—she's preparing herself for the return of Jesus.
- **The Government of God Is Increasing** Jesus' rule is expanding, even if we can't always see it. Our prayers are pushing it forward.
- **History Belongs to the Intercessors** Those who pray shape the future. You're not reactive—you're prophetic.
- **We Must Fix Our Eyes on the Eternal** Don't get stuck in temporary disappointment. Lift your eyes to what's coming.

Journaling Questions

This chapter reframes your purpose. You're not just praying for revival—you're preparing the earth for the return of the King. You're not just interceding for a better week—you're aligning history with heaven. Let these journaling moments anchor you in the long game. God sees the end from the beginning, and your "yes" matters more than you know.

As you journal, ask the Lord to open your eyes to the eternal. Let Him show you the ripple effects of your hidden faithfulness. Let Him ignite your hope with His promises. And most of all, let Him reaffirm that He's writing a story, and you're a critical part of it.

God's Endgame in My Life

How does knowing that God's glory will fill the earth shift the way I live and pray today?

_____
_____
_____
_____

My Role in His Story

In what ways am I participating in God's eternal narrative through my obedience?

_____
_____
_____
_____
_____
_____

Endurance in the Process

What causes me to grow weary or lose sight of the bigger picture, and how can I refocus?

_____
_____
_____
_____
_____
_____

Preparing for His Return

What does it look like practically for me to live as a bride making herself ready?

_____
_____
_____
_____
_____
_____

Faith in the Unseen

What do I believe God is doing through my unseen, unrewarded moments of obedience?

_____
_____
_____
_____
_____

Actionable Steps

Cultivate Eternal Vision
Take time this week to meditate on Scriptures about the return of Jesus and the coming kingdom. Let His endgame shape your daily decisions.

Equip Yourself with Prophetic Perspective
Journal or speak aloud three ways your current season is preparing you for God's future purposes.

Engage in Intercession with Purpose
When you pray, speak out God's promises for the earth. Declare His coming glory. Pray with the end in mind.

Personal Reflection

This chapter reminds me that I'm not living for today—I'm living for forever. Every act of faithfulness, every whisper in prayer, every sacrifice I've made—it's going somewhere. God is weaving my life into a tapestry of glory. And when I feel like quitting, I have to remember that the story isn't over. There's still more glory to come.

I want to live like someone who believes Jesus is coming. I want to pray like someone who knows her voice helps shape history. I want to burn with vision—not just for personal breakthrough, but for global awakening. I may not see it all now, but one day, every knee will bow and every tongue confess that Jesus is Lord.

Will I live for the long story or the short gain? Will I let God use my hidden years to build eternal things? Will I align my heart with His vision for the nations, no matter the cost?

Closing Prayer: *Lord, give me vision for the long story. Help me see beyond the moment and live for eternity. Let me partner with You to fill the earth with Your glory. Keep me steady when it's hard, faithful when it's unseen, and joyful in the labor. Come, Lord Jesus—let Your kingdom come through me. Amen.*

Chapter 12

What Does This Look Like Today?

"And it shall come to pass in the last days, says God, that I will pour out of My Spirit on all flesh; your sons and your daughters shall prophesy, your young men shall see visions, your old men shall dream dreams." (Acts 2:17, NKJV)

I remember standing in a church in Dallas, Texas, watching a group of high school students lead worship with tears streaming down their faces. It wasn't a performance—it was presence. Something holy had broken in. There were no celebrity pastors, no lights or stage tricks. Just a simple group of burning hearts, releasing a sound that could only come from the altar of devotion. And I thought to myself, "This is what it looks like." This is what revival in real life sounds like. Ordinary people giving themselves to extraordinary surrender.

We've talked about identity, intercession, and intimacy throughout this journey. But many are left asking: what does it actually look like to walk this out? How do I give my life to prayer, fasting, worship, and loving Jesus in the midst of jobs, families, and daily responsibilities? The answer is not in escaping culture—it's in burning for God within it. God is raising up communities of presence and individuals with fire in their bones who live every moment aware of heaven's activity.

This chapter anchors the call of intercession in reality. It brings the prophetic life out of the clouds and into the kitchen, the classroom, the business meeting. It shows us that revival isn't locked to a pulpit or a platform. Revival is when the Spirit breaks in wherever you are, because you've built an altar there. And from that altar, the fragrance of your life draws the eyes of heaven to earth.

You don't have to quit your job to live this life—you just have to let God consume everything you are, wherever you are. Are you ready to burn in the ordinary until it becomes holy?

Focus Point

"I will pour out of My Spirit on all flesh…" (Acts 2:17, NKJV)

This verse destroys the myth that revival is reserved for the elite or the ultra-spiritual. God's Spirit is not confined to a temple or title. His promise is to pour out on *all flesh*—sons, daughters, young, old, male, female, across every barrier and border. This is the reality we must live in today: we are all candidates for divine outpouring, if we are willing to yield.

Main Theme

This chapter grounds the intercessor's call in daily life. It paints a picture of what it looks like to burn for God in our current context—not just as full-time ministers but as faithful sons and daughters who create space for heaven in the everyday. We are called to live lives that host God's presence, ignite prayer, and transform atmospheres in our homes, churches, and communities. Revival isn't future—it's now.

"Revival looks like you, fully surrendered, wherever you are."

Key Scriptures

- *"You are the light of the world. A city that is set on a hill cannot be hidden."* (Matthew 5:14, NKJV)
- *"But you, when you pray, go into your room, and when you have shut your door, pray to your Father who is in the secret place."* (Matthew 6:6, NKJV)
- *"Do not be slothful in zeal, be fervent in spirit, serve the Lord."* (Romans 12:11, NKJV)

Key Points

- **Revival Is Local and Personal** You don't have to travel to experience God. Build an altar right where you are.
- **The Secret Place Fuels Public Impact** Public authority comes from private surrender. Hidden intercession shapes visible change.
- **God Uses the Unqualified** He pours His Spirit on *all flesh*, not just spiritual professionals. You are not disqualified.
- **Communities of Presence Are Rising** God is building houses of prayer and worship in ordinary places filled with extraordinary hunger.
- **Devotion Is the New Normal** What once seemed radical—fasting, prayer, night-and-day worship—is becoming the baseline for surrendered lives.
- **Revival Requires Simplicity** The more complicated your life, the harder it is to burn. Simplicity makes room for fire.
- **Every Environment Can Be Holy Ground** Your job, home, or school becomes sacred when you host God there.

Journaling Questions

This chapter is about living it out. Not just talking about revival but becoming revival. Journaling here invites you to take stock of your current routines, your daily spaces, and your internal posture toward God. Where is your fire burning? Where is it flickering? What spaces need to become altars again?

As you reflect, don't aim for perfection—aim for presence. God's not asking for flawless performance. He's asking for a heart that says, "Here I am. Consume me." Let this section clarify your next steps. Not just in theory, but in practice.

Your Personal Altar

Where in my daily life have I built altars of devotion that host God's presence?

_____
_____
_____
_____

Simplicity for the Sake of Fire

What distractions need to be removed so I can burn more consistently?

_____
_____
_____
_____
_____
_____

Your Calling in the Chaos

How can I carry God's presence into my job, school, or family with greater intentionality?

_____
_____
_____
_____
_____
_____

Community and Fire

Am I connected to others who are burning? If not, what steps can I take to find that community?

_____
_____
_____
_____
_____
_____

Making Revival Practical

What does it look like for me to prioritize prayer and intimacy with God in this season?

_____
_____
_____
_____
_____
_____

Actionable Steps

Cultivate a Set Time and Place for Prayer
Create a consistent rhythm of meeting with God. Whether it's ten minutes or an hour, be faithful to show up and burn.

Equip Your Environment
Turn your home or workspace into a sanctuary. Play worship. Keep Scripture visible. Invite the Holy Spirit to dwell with you.

Engage with Like-Minded Believers
Find a local or online prayer group. Don't burn alone—fire spreads faster in community.

Personal Reflection

This chapter feels like the crescendo of everything we've been building toward. It takes all the theology, all the identity, all the fire and brings it into the kitchen, the office, the car ride. I realize that the greatest revival I may ever host won't happen from a platform—it will happen in my living room. God's not waiting on a move—He's looking for a vessel.

I want my life to look like revival. I want my daily routines to be saturated with His Spirit. I want my family to know what it's like to live with someone who burns for God. I may not have the loudest voice, but I can have the deepest flame. And that flame can light up every space I enter.

Am I willing to let my normal become holy? Will I live each day as a chance to host heaven? Will I be the revival I've been praying to see?

Closing Prayer: *Lord, let revival begin with me. Take my ordinary and make it holy. Let my home become a sanctuary, my life an altar, and my heart a resting place for You. Fill me with fresh fire and help me to live a surrendered life wherever I go. Let my yes ignite others and let my obedience prepare the way for Your glory. Amen.*

About the Author

About Corey Russell

Corey Russell's passion is to awaken prayer across the earth. He travels

nationally and internationally, imparting the spirit of prayer and awakening a hunger for revival.

He has written nine books, released six prayer albums, and is discipling thousands in his online school coreyrussellonline.com, and

training preachers in his messenger mentorship. He is on the pastoral team at House Denver in Denver, CO, where he lives with his wife and three daughters.

———

Harrison House is a Spirit-filled, Word of Faith Christian publisher dedicated to spreading the message of faith, hope, and love through our wide range of inspiring publications. Committed to the messages that highlight the power of the Word and Spirit, we provide books, devotionals, and study guides that empower believers to live victorious, faith-filled lives.

Our resources are designed to help readers grow spiritually, strengthen their faith, and experience the transformative power of God's Word. Harrison House is passionate about equipping Christians with the tools they need to fulfill their divine purpose and impact the world for Christ.

www.ingramcontent.com/pod-product-compliance
Lightning Source LLC
Chambersburg PA
CBHW080839230426
43665CB00021B/2888